debt-free
IN 3 SIMPLE STEPS

PETER FRITZ
peterfritz.co

debt-free

Copyright © 2019 Peter Fritz
All rights reserved.
ISBN: 9781798607749

DEDICATION

To mum and dad, for teaching me the value of hard work and good habits. And to Amy, Sarah and Tommy - I hope never have to read this book.

ACKNOWLEDGMENTS

Writing a book is hard. Writing a book you're proud of is *really* hard.

I have a lot of people to thank for helping me knock this into shape. Here are some of them.

Steven Pressfield - for your timely and heartfelt encouragement

Seth Godin - for showing me the power of generous emotional labour

James Altucher - for convincing me to reinvent myself

Laura Belgray & Marie Forleo - for giving me decent writing chops

Jonathan Mead - for getting me started on this journey in the first place

Scott & Chelsea Dinsmore - for inspiring ordinary people to be legends

Corbett Barr - for giving me the tools and mindset to blaze my own trail

Steph Crowder - for being a champion of endless encouragement

Ken W. Fife - for 20 years of mentorship, and for leading by example

Michael Yardney - for giving it to me straight, year after year

CONTENTS

Chapter 1	The Beginning	9
Chapter 2	How Did I Get Here?	13
Chapter 3	Don't Do a Budget	21
	Step 1	22
	Step 2	24
	Step 3	26
	The Spreadsheet That'll Set you Free	28
Chapter 4	Let the Killing Begin	31
	What if I Can't Repay my Debt?	34
	Your Mortgage	36
	Tax Debt	38
Chapter 5	Mastering Debt	39
	Good Debt	44
	Why is Real Estate so Good for Debt?	46
	Bad Debt	48
	Credit Cards	50
	Lifestyle Purchases	52
	Ugly Debt	54
Chapter 6	Breathe Again	56
	A Final Word (warning)	58
	A Small Favor	60
	Additional Resources	61
	About the Peter	63
	Glossary	65

One of the biggest killers is *stress*.

Debt is often the catalyst.

1 | THE BEGINNING - DECISION TIME

If you had to pick one thing that's kept you awake at nights, what would it be? I'm guessing you'd say *debts*, or *bills!* Okay, you might say, *Jessica Alba* or *Tom Hardy*... No judgment, here.

I've done both. Not the Jessica Alba thing, but the 'debts' and 'bills' things - laying in bed, running through them over and over again. One night I became so paralyzed with worry I had a heart attack. You haven't lived till you've had one of those.

Maybe you've dreamed of winning the lottery. If you have, the most appealing part was probably the dream of living debt-free.

When used correctly, debt is actually very good for you. The trouble is, most of us use it for stuff that sends us into an abyss of misery and stress. That's exactly what *I* did.

Centuries ago, things were different. Folks didn't have to deal with this sh*t. Instead, the threats they faced were big toothy animals or other tribes that wanted to eat their children. Back then, people would fight their threats head-on or they'd run from them. But you can't do either with debt. That's why the problem is so debilitating; that's why it paralyzes people and breaks apart marriages.

So in this book I'm going to teach you what to do about it, using the methods *I* used after a painful and costly divorce. These are practical steps you can take right away to lift the fog and breathe again.

I must warn you, though - this journey is not for wishful thinkers, excuse makers or status-hungry Jones-pleasers. It's more like a killing spree. To vanquish your debts, you'll need to be properly armed and trigger-happy.

Perhaps your experience says otherwise, but life is *not* meant to be a continuous struggle of debt and worry. Let me show you why.

TWO

Tackling this problem requires a three-step process, and I'll lay it all out for you in a minute, but before you jump ahead, there are two things you must do.

THINGS

1

Ask, "How exactly did I get here?"

Setting aside circumstances beyond our control, there are always fundamental issues that drive our behavior. You're in this position today because of decisions you made and actions you took in the years before. You'll need to address the cause of those decisions or else you'll you slip back into debt once we're done here.

2

Decide right now that you'll never return to this state.

Carrying *consumer* debt - the kind that makes you poor - is terrible for your health. It also poisons your relationships and sucks the energy out of everything you do.

The ripple effect is up there with alcoholism and drug addiction. Promise yourself that once you're done with this, **you are done.**

2 | HOW DID I GET HERE?

I used to have a spending problem, but I convinced myself I was having fun, so it wasn't *really* a problem. At first, this was true. And then it wasn't. I started worrying about money, and each time I thought about buying something, I became filled with anxiety and dread.

It took me many years to learn that the root cause of all this was a deeply entrenched and fundamentally flawed belief system that had me seeking fulfillment and purpose in all the wrong places.

I'd fallen into a common trap – spending money on crap I didn't need to compensate for the lack of purpose in my life. The subsequent burden of paying for it led to stress, which made me buy *more* stuff as a reward for all the extra work I was doing to pay for it.

Yes, I had beautiful children, gainful employment and a modicum of freedom to do stuff I enjoyed, but the more I rewarded myself the more I became a slave to consumption. It was a zero sum game.

Here are some of the dumb things I did.

- *I bought fancy cars to feel 'successful'.*
- *I had lots of hobbies but never the time to engage in them.*
- *I accumulated toys that embodied adventure and excitement, yet couldn't get away from work to use them.*
- *I took expensive holidays but couldn't relax because of the cost.*
- *I only wore Versace ties, even though I looked like a wanker.*
- *I ate at upscale restaurants in the casino district, despite the food and service being no better than places costing half as much.*

debt-free

The simple fact is, I'd forgotten the true source of happiness.

Looking back on that period reminds me of the movie, "Eat, Pray, Love" (yes, I admit it). In a scene at a traditional Italian barbershop, Luca Spaghetti says to the American tourist played by Julia Roberts,

"The trouble with you Americans is you know 'entertainment', but you don't know 'pleasure'!"

This is true for many of us. Most of what we consume is nothing more than a distraction. It's *entertainment*, not pleasure.

Entertainment is a fleeting experience, like a cheeseburger. Pleasure, though, is something you feel at a deeper level, and with none of the follow-on guilt. Like Wagyu steak.

And like teenagers who express their insecurities with violence, promiscuity or vanity, thoughtless consumption is just a *symptom* of a deeper problem.

Most of what we buy is nothing more than a distraction. **It's entertainment, not pleasure.**

What's driving your behavior?

With honest examination, you can trace the origins of your spending habits quite easily. It usually boils down to one or more of these sources:

1. **Your parents' behavior** – what they valued, the relationship they had with money and the meaning they attached to it – whether it was a scarcity mindset, their desire to keep up with the neighbors or a 'money isn't important' philosophy.

2. **Your peers** – where they live, what they wear, what they drive, where their kids are schooled, where they holiday in the summer, and so on.

3. **Marketing messages** – how easily you believe the bullsh*t you read and see on TV; whether you devour the junk mail or toss it straight into the bin, and how easily marketing messages trigger 'new shiny syndrome'.

These sources have one thing in common – modeling. The trouble is, they're modeling the wrong group; the one that'll keep you broke.

You become the average of the people you spend the most time with. If these people have a reckless and unbalanced relationship with money, then in all likelihood, so will you.

If they're echoing the marketing channels you also consume (social media, television, radio, magazines, billboards, shopping websites), then you're screwed.

Remember, broke people stay broke by living like they're rich.

Make a few changes and the burden will begin to lift.

The time to fix all this is <u>today</u>. If you think the last ten years flew by, just watch what happens with the *next* ten! Before you know it, you'll be OLD.

Don't waste any more time on stupid excuses because, as I always say, *your biggest problem is you think you have time.* You don't.

I know it's hard to accept (even though you know it's true), but there is a world of pleasure out there that won't cost you a cracker.

The best things in life don't come with a label stitched to them or a brand name emblazoned on the front for your equally afflicted friends to admire. Many of the best things are priceless ***and free.***

If you want to start thinking deliberately about your spending, I recommend you do these four things:

1. Quit all TV consumption that has advertising. We disconnected ours from free-to-air and cable on May 1st, 2007. We have a home cinema with a decent collection of movies, and an Apple TV box for new release stuff, but we probably watch around 3-5 hours a week. And no ads.

2. Look closely at the people you spend the most time with and ask yourself if their lives are worth copying. Are they simply doing what you're doing and trying to keep up with their own Joneses? Are they genuinely happy, fulfilled, content and excited about life or do they talk about 'stuff' all the time – the kind you have to pay for?

3. Think objectively about the way you were raised, then put your parents' beliefs into context. They are **their** beliefs. They don't have to be *yours*.

4. Decide to learn about money and how you can use it to improve your life rather than *distract you from it*.

By the way, none of this applies if you have genuine issues around income deprivation (job loss, family illness or other personal issues that limit your earning capacity), or an addiction of some kind.

Those kinds of challenges require very different advice, so please don't be offended by the narrow scope of this chapter.

Alright, let's move on.

3 | DON'T DO A BUDGET

I've done lots of budgets and I hated every one of them.

Budgets are like diets. They're smothered in optimism and that's why they rarely work. And that's why you're not going to do one here - not in the traditional sense, anyway.

Budgets also fail to address the disconnect between your spending and your long-term objectives and values. In other words, they're not driven by anything other than a desire to spend less.

Because of this, you slip back into the same old patterns, spending money on things that create more of the same pain.

The 3-Step Process That Works

Writing a budget is unpleasant, I know. First, it requires that you document every dollar you spend. Second, it means setting limits on spending based on optimistic expectations of your discipline levels.

It's the second part where things fall apart, because you always think you're more disciplined than you really are. If you were, you probably wouldn't be in this mess to begin with.

Documenting what you spend is impossible to avoid (sorry), but the second step (the bit that never works) is for the birds.

Here's the method I used to kill $140k in consumer debt. It works.

1. Determine what you spend per month.
2. Answer key questions about each expense.
3. Reduce, substitute and cull based on **facts**, not wishful thinking.

debt-free

1 Record what you spend.

The best way to complete this mind-numbing task is to make all your purchases with a credit or debit card (depending on your level of discipline).

Do this for at least a month (preferably two) then pull down a report of all your transactions from your Internet banking into a spreadsheet and group them into categories. Some examples of these might include: groceries, dining out, office lunches, phone, utilities,

loan payments, transport, entertainment, personal care items, etc..

Your banking software will probably create the categories for you but many of these will be wrong. Define them yourself and edit your spreadsheet accordingly.

Alternatively, keep a journal of every dollar spent – either with pen and paper or via a simple app on your phone. Check the iTunes store or Google Play for something suitable. The main thing is, you MUST know what you're spending first.

Once you have at least a month's worth of transactions, determine all your recurring expenses that run on longer cycles like insurances, school fees, association/club memberships, subscriptions, vehicle registrations and so on.

Calculate the monthly value of these and add them to the list. For example, an annual expense of $765 would equal $63.75 per month.

After you've grouped everything into appropriate categories, you'll see exactly where your money goes. This can be liberating *and* frightening - because for perhaps the first time, you'll see where you're blowing a disproportionate amount of money. But likewise, you'll spot the low hanging fruit where you can get some quick wins.

I know this part is unpleasant, but like any bad habit, the first step towards a resolution is admitting you have one. By revealing exactly what you're spending and where, you'll know what you're working with. **The pendulum of control now swings back to you.**

If you complete this step, you'll be ahead of two-thirds of the population, so pat yourself on the back.

Armed with your total monthly spending, you can now get to work on step two.

Answer these questions.

The first step is difficult to fake because even though you *could* leave a few bits out, the facts are the facts, and hiding them would be pointless and stupid.

Step two, on the other hand, is *easy* to fake or gloss over. But for it to work, you **must** be completely honest. This step involves introspection and interpretation, but most of all, **decisions**. Go through each expense and ask yourself these questions:

- Why am I buying this? Necessity? Status? Convenience?
- Is it something I can't live without or is it a financial burden that I can eliminate?
- Does this expense bring me closer to freedom or push it away?
- Can I get this item cheaper elsewhere?
- Can I substitute it for something that's just as effective (or pleasurable) for less money or no money at all?
- Does the benefit I get from this justify the cost?
- What would this expense amount to if I invested it at 7% per annum, compounded for ten years? As an example, $500 a month, compounded at 7% pm over 10 years is $86,500!

Another thing - you'll probably see plenty of **one-off** expenses on your list - things you don't ordinarily buy. These will pop up all the time. Some are seasonal, especially around the holidays, but others are indulgences that you can and **should** reduce.

Include all of them on the list, but reduce their value by 50%. We're not doing a budget here, but a good way to look at this is, each time an opportunity for a one-off expenses arises (especially if it's an indulgence), be very mindful of what you're doing.

Tell yourself you're cutting all one-off expenses in half, and try to do exactly that. Our goal with our spending is to be *intentional* about it.

debt-free

Reduce, substitute, cull.

Decide what you can reduce, what you can substitute for something cheaper (or free), and what you can eliminate (cull).

This step will require research but believe me, this is **one of the fastest ways to make money.** By reducing your expenses, by substituting costly ones, and by culling the ones you can live without, you'll be giving yourself an instant pay rise.

Once you start applying this windfall to your debts and they begin to tumble, you'll reduce your monthly costs further. **Each round will deliver another pay rise!**

As you decide what to do with each one (reduce, substitute or cull), write the *new* values against your expenses (zero if you're culling them) in a separate column called 'New Cost PM (per month)'.

Once you're done, you'll now have a total amount that you're going to spend maintaining the lifestyle you're comfortable with.

Hopefully, you're left with a **surplus** (net monthly income less monthly expenses). You will now deposit this surplus amount into a separate bank account each and every pay day.

This is what you'll use to kill off your debts. We're going to call it The Killing Fund, and it will to be your savior.

Set up an automatic direct debit from your main account (the one that receives your pay) into The Killing Fund for the surplus mentioned above, each time you're paid.

As soon as you complete this third step, I promise you'll already feel better about your financial future. You'll begin to develop confidence in your ability to shape and direct your life in ways that, till now, may have been out of reach.

The next page illustrates how your spreadsheet might look. I've taken the ugly CSV file I downloaded from my Internet banking and prettied it up a bit so it's easier on the eyes.

You'll see I've also added a few of columns for totaling my expense categories, adding comments against expenses and revising the item amounts where appropriate (after reducing, substituting or culling).

This spreadsheet will set you free.

Now we get to the really important part! Skip this step and you *will* die a lonely, miserable, penniless person - with badly-stained teeth and a leaky bladder.

I know you don't want to do this. I know you're already thinking of ways around it, but please don't. You came to me remember? Do what I'm telling you even if the thought of it makes you physically ill.

What you see here is a combination of real entries from my Internet banking download and some fictitious entries to illustrate how this whole thing works. I don't have any debts except for real estate, so I've had to make a few up.

Be sure you define the categories in a way that's logical to you, and don't rely on your downloaded transactions to define them for you because they're often wrong. The 'Category Subs' are only there to illustrate which categories consume the most money.

The 'Notes' column is where you record your decisions based off the questions in Step 2, or just general comments about that particular expense. The last column reflects the adjusted values after those decisions are made. There's a link to a copy of this spreadsheet at the end of this book, so you can use that as a guide.

Your goal is to have a **monthly surplus** (the last cell) to deposit into The Killing Fund. If you're paid weekly, multiply the surplus by 12 then divide by 52 so you'll know how much to deposit into the fund each week. This is the amount you will <u>automatically</u> credit to The Killing Fund every pay day. You'll then put that money on the debt you're currently killing. Got it? If you haven't, re-read this page and study the spreadsheet till you have.

I'm just a spreadsheet. I don't bite... :-)

Date	Expense	Curr $ PM	Category	Category Subs	Notes	New $ PM
1/1/17	Car Loan 1	-$500.00	Loan		9% | Bal: $7k	-$500.00
1/1/17	Car Loan 2	-$850.00	Loan		9% | Bal: $15k	-$850.00
1/1/17	Store Card	-$300.00	Loan		22% | Bal: $4k	-$300.00
1/1/17	Credit Card	-$400.00	Loan	-$2,050.00	18% | Bal: $6k	-$400.00
1/1/17	Home Loan	-$1,500.00	PPR Mortgage	-$1,500.00	5% | Bal: $300k	-$1,500.00
1/1/17	Investment Loan 1	-$1,000.00	Invest Loan		5% | Bal: $250k	-$1,000.00
1/1/17	Investment Loan 2	-$900.00	Invest Loan	-$1,900.00	5% | Bal: $220k	-$900.00
Annual	Car 1 Insurance	-$65.00	Transport		Still the cheapest	-$65.00
Annual	Car 2 Insurance	-$87.00	Transport		Still the cheapest	-$87.00
Annual	Car 1 Registration	-$60.00	Transport		Can't change this.	-$60.00
Annual	Car 2 Registration	-$60.00	Transport		Can't change this.	-$60.00
21/1/17	AMEX 7-ELEVEN 1326 ST. KILDA	-$58.98	Transport		Cannot reduce	-$58.98
6/1/17	AMEX CALTEX GREENVALE	-$34.98	Transport		Cannot reduce	-$34.98
26/1/17	CSAND PTY LTD WESTMEADOWS	-$126.22	Transport	-$220.18	Cannot reduce	-$126.22
31/1/17	AMEX DIGITAL PACIFIC PTY LTD	$20.75	Utilities		Lowest suitable level	$20.75
13/1/17	AMEX TELSTRA Internet	-$150.89	Utilities		Best plan for us.	-$150.89
16/1/17	AMEX TELSTRA Mobile Phones	-$261.66	Utilities		SUBSTITUTE (XYZ Co.)	-$100.00
23/1/17	MOMENTUM MELBOURNE GAS	-$192.69	Utilities		Already the cheapest	-$192.69
23/1/17	MOMENTUM MELBOURNE ELEC	-$247.32	Utilities		Already the cheapest	-$192.69
Quarterly	Hume City Council (Rates)	-$251.50	Utilities		Can't change this.	-$251.50
3/1/17	YARRA VALLEY WATER MITCHAM	$124.50	Utilities	-$1,085.03	Can't change this.	$124.50
25/1/17	CONVERTKIT.COM 29.00 USD	-$38.50	Biz Expense		Lowest level avail	-$38.50
10/1/17	AMEX ADOBE *CREATIVE CLOUD	-$63.79	Biz Expense		Need this.	-$63.79
31/1/17	AMEX FACEBK *KLGTJCE6F2	-$176.48	Biz Expense		Experimenting	-$176.48
7/1/17	AMEX HARVEST NY 129.60 USD	-$13.00	Biz Expense		Need this.	-$13.00
23/1/17	AMEX MAILCHIMP 10.00 USD	-$13.50	Biz Expense		CULL	$0.00
7/1/17	AMEX XERO AUSTRALIA P/L XERO	-$100.00	Biz Expense	-$405.27	REDUCE (to base lev)	-$50.00
5/1/17	ST COLUMBAS COLLEGE ESSENDON	-$1,554.80	Education		Can't change this.	-$1,554.80
Annual	CAMPION EDUCATION NUNA	-$150.00	Education	-$1,704.80	School Books	-$150.00
29/1/17	APPLE ITUNES STORE SYDNEY	-$13.98	Entertainment		OK	-$13.98
21/1/17	LUNA PARK MELBOURNE ST KILDA	-$139.85	Entertainment	-$153.83	One-off expense.	-$70.00
7/1/17	AMEX LOCCITANE HIGHPOINT NL	-$124.00	Personal Care		One-off expense.	-$62.00
7/1/17	AMEX REBEL SPORTS HIGHPOINT	-$40.98	Personal Care	-$164.98	One-off expense.	-$20.00
27/1/17	AMEX KOBE JONES MELBOURNE	-$71.50	Dining Out		OK	-$71.50
28/1/17	BETTYS BURGERS MELBOURNE	-$24.50	Dining Out	-$96.00	OK	-$24.50
25/1/17	AMEX AUSTRALIA FOR UNHCR	-$50.00	Donations		OK	-$50.00
2/1/17	AMEX MAKE-A-WISH FOUNDATION	-$33.00	Donations		OK	-$33.00
6/1/17	DEAF SERVICES ALDERLEY QLD	-$20.00	Donations	-$103.00	OK	-$20.00
4/1/17	AMEX COLES GREENVALE	-$23.35	Groceries		OK	-$23.35
20/1/17	AMEX COLES GREENVALE	-$124.78	Groceries		OK	-$124.78
26/1/17	AMEX WOOLWORTHS 3145 NIDDRIE	-$123.78	Groceries	-$271.91	OK	-$123.78
25/1/17	AMEX SLADE PHARMACY WAVERLY	-$36.04	Health		One-off expense.	-$18.00
16/1/17	TAL LIFE LIMITED SYDNEY	-$74.12	Health		Reducing each year.	-$74.12
23/1/17	LEAKE ST CLINIC ESSENDON	-$75.00	Health		One-off expense.	-$38.00
1/1/17	PURE ORTHODONTICS MOONEE P	-$125.00	Health	-$310.16	Will end May 17	-$125.00
1/1/17	AMEX KMART AIRPORT WEST	-$126.99	Retail shopping		OK	-$126.99
7/1/17	AMEX MYER HIGHPOINT	-$249.75	Retail shopping		One-off. Clothes.	-$125.00
28/1/17	BETTS KIDS MARIBYRNONG	-$99.99	Retail shopping		One-off. School shoes.	-$50.00
17/1/17	PAYPAL *MSX289-DCA 734.98 USD	-$981.43	Retail shopping	-$1,458.16	One-off expense.	$0.00
	Current Cost TOTAL	-$11,569.10			New Cost TOTAL	-$9,925.27
					Net Income PM	$11,000.00
					SURPLUS PM	$1,074.73

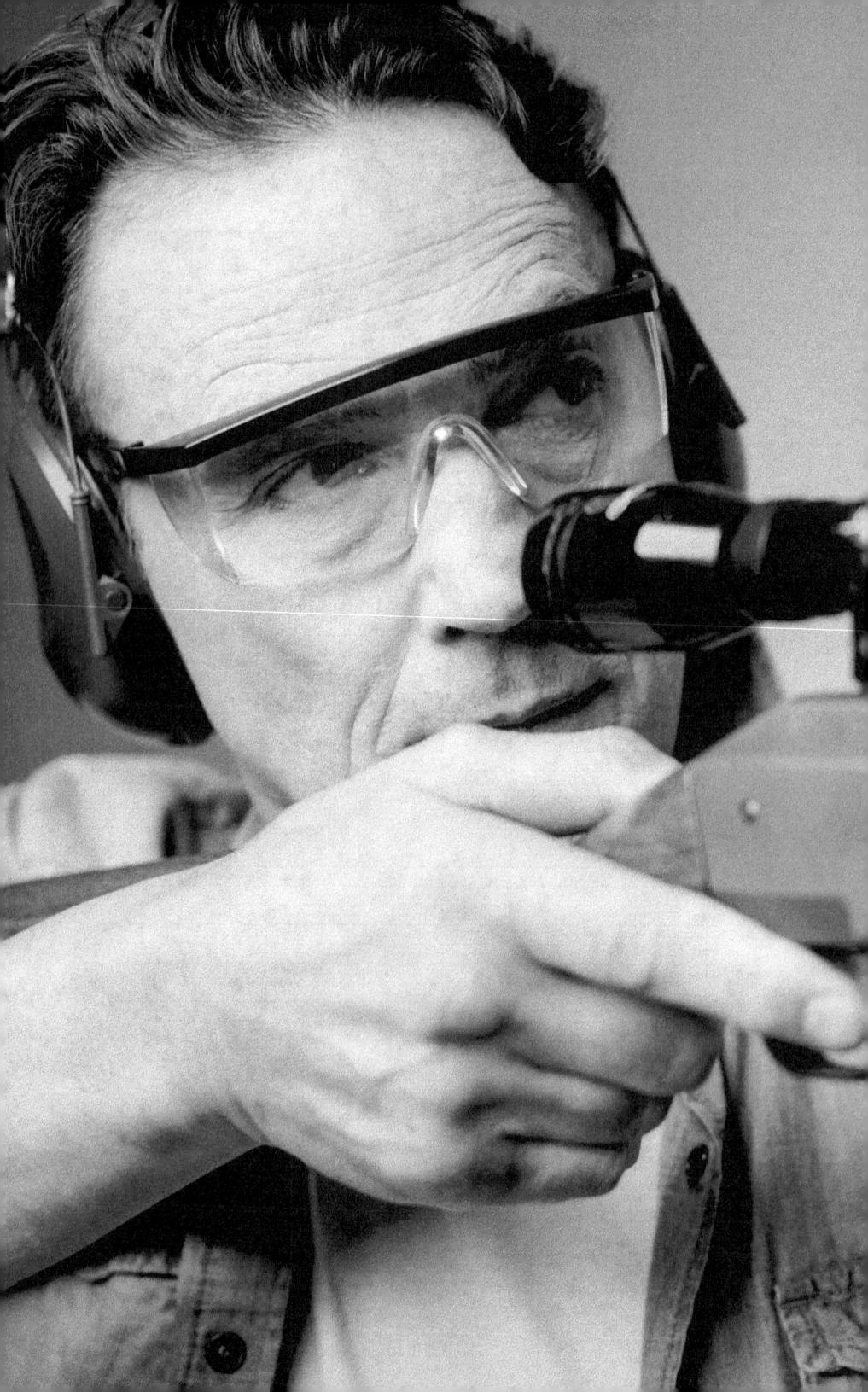

4 | LET THE KILLING BEGIN

Priority One

A lot of experts will tell you that to pay down your debts, you must kill them in descending order - from the one with the highest interest rate, down to the lowest. And technically, they'd be right.

But, what you need right now is an easy victory or two. So I recommend going after the debt with the **smallest outstanding balance first**. Kill that one, get a taste for it, then decide what's next.

Also, a key element of this process is the immutable law called **delayed gratification**.

Remember the spending analysis we did in the last chapter? Well, if you're serious about this process, everything you *want* at the moment will be placed on hold. Pay TV, dining out, holidays, booze, clothes; in fact, anything you don't <u>need</u> should be culled.

The pleasure you get from these things won't outweigh the pain of staying in debt. If you have to keep one of them, go cheap. Get your red wine from one of the big on-line discounters, or pay for your movies or TV shows one at a time and limit your consumption. We're going on a killing spree, here. Only the essentials matter.

In fact, turning away from the TV altogether frees up a huge amount of time. Why not invest that time in learning how to sell your unwanted stuff on eBay? Or learn to create a small side-hustle. There's no reason why you can't attack this problem from both ends, you know. Save money, make money.

The First Victim

Now that you're all set up, it time to start pouring every available dollar into the first debt - the one with the smallest balance.

Also, do it more often than the standard monthly cycle if it's appropriate. In other words, if your job pays you weekly, use all of the automatic weekly payment that goes into The Killing Fund on this debt every week.

You'll want to reduce the balance upon which interest is calculated as quickly as possible, and increasing the payment frequency can help with this.

Remember, this payment is <u>in addition</u> to the standard payment you already make on this debt. This rule applies to every debt from here on. Make sure you focus on only ONE debt until it's gone.

What happens next is glorious. You'll have already proven that you can change, and that will give you a thrill. Do this for a few payment cycles and you'll achieve something few others do - you'll learn how to swim upstream.

Remember that most people live by *circumstance*, not conviction. By deciding how to behave; by deliberately eschewing bad debt and the burden it creates, you'll immediately join a wonderful minority who live with purpose, **on purpose**.

Also, a great thing about this process is, it resets your pleasure threshold (what you think you *need* in order to feel pleasure), and it recalibrates your pain/reward ratio – the amount of debt you're prepared to carry to deliver a 'reward'.

One, two, watch them fall.

Once you've vanquished your first debt, you'll now have those payments freed up for the next one.

Your regular payments into The Killing Fund should now include the original savings from chapter three plus the 'standard' payments you were making on the first debt. This is your second pay rise.

Congratulations, you're on your way!

If you've managed to knock over your first debt in less than six months, I suggest following the same principle again with debt number two and pouring all of the money from The Killing Fund into your *next smallest* debt. Momentum is everything here.

After killing your second debt, you'll feel a whole lot better than you did before setting out on this journey. The mental burden will have lifted and the future will become a promise you can start to foretell with greater certainty.

Armed with the additional cash you've liberated from your first two debts, you'll now be in a position to swing for the fences, and tackle your remaining debts in descending order from the highest interest rate to the lowest. These might be credit cards, store cards or a personal loan. Apply **all** of The Killing Fund to each remaining debt one at a time, until they're all dead.

Emboldened by your progress and hopefully, with a new perspective on wasteful spending, you'll plow through any remaining debts with enthusiasm and speed.

What if I can't repay my debts?

If you simply can't repay a debt, there *are* other options. Local laws and regulations vary from country to country, but bankruptcy and debt negotiation are sometimes valid choices.

Unsecured debts like credit and store cards that are more than 90 days overdue are often sold to collection agencies for a fraction of their face value. If one of your debts progresses to this stage, you'll probably have to accept a black mark against your credit rating.

This is called a 'default' and it will impact your borrowing capacity (even your eligibility for a phone account) for at least a few years.

The upshot is, you'll be able to negotiate the settlement of your debt for a substantially lower amount. If you can secure the funds from another source (equity in your home, the sale of assets or a family member) and settle the debt quickly, you might even be able to request the removal of your default listing.

Banks can be surprisingly helpful, too. Many of them have a structured application process for debt reduction, and if your situation's genuine, they may *reduce* your debt with them. Following my post-divorce unpleasantness, two banks agreed to reduce my

debts to them by over 40%. It was a life-saver.

Your options might include a reduced settlement value (to be paid in full), an interest-free repayment period, or an extended repayment schedule where the term of the loan is extended by months or years (which reduces the size of your monthly repayments).

If you have a home loan in arrears (you're behind on payments), you might be able to switch to interest-only payments for a few years. In all likelihood, the growth in value of your home will take care of most (if not all) of the principal component you're *not* repaying. After all, most of the repayments in the first 15 years of a typical home loan are the interest component, anyway.

If you decide to explore the bankruptcy route, just know that it isn't as simple as waving the white flag and hitting the reset button. Part of the procedure may include garnisheeing your salary for a portion of your outstanding debts.

When you become bankrupt, a trustee is assigned to you, and they manage your financial affairs for the life of your bankruptcy (three years in Australia). They also impose limitations on the assets you can hold, even the value of the car you drive.

You might see bankruptcy as an easy way out, and for some, it's the *only* way out. But the effects can drag on - impacting future credit applications, employment and the loss of cherished assets.

'Phoenixing' (the intentional transfer of assets from an indebted company to a new company to avoid paying creditors, tax or employee entitlements) was popular with small businesses until the Australian Government decided to focus on this activity. Intentional 'phoenixing' is now a jail-able offence.

Paying off your Mortgage

A lot of people want to own their own home. Personally, I don't see the value in it. To me, it misses the biggest opportunity most of us have for leverage and wealth creation.

Your home is more than just a roof over your head. It's also the best source of the cheapest finance available - equity.

Years ago, one of Australia's major banks started promoting their line-of-credit products to non-investors. Want a holiday, a new car or a boat? "Equity, mate!" People went nuts for it.

Before 'Equity mate!' Joe Average spent $660 a month for five years on a new $30,000 car, and repaid a total of $39,000. Now he could put it 'on the house' for just $230 a month and repay $69,000 over 25 years instead! Assuming interest rates never went up...

I'd rather buy real estate with my equity, and let my money make money. Every mortgage I've had has been an interest-only one. Usually you can't do this on your principal place of residence forever (the house you live in), unless you switch banks every five years.

The equity on my properties comes from the growth in value, not my principal repayments. And since I never speculate with real estate, my properties have always trended upward.

Rather than applying a principal payment to the mortgage, I prefer to use that money to buy another house. That way, I have not one, but two houses growing in value.

This is a whole other subject, and I recommend you check the Additional Resources section at the back of this book and get the tools you need to master it. You'll also find a useful equity calculator to download back there.

But suffice to say, paying off my house before I'm 70 does nothing to improve my life. Reinvesting the accumulated equity in my home **plus** the principal payments I'd otherwise waste *does* improve my life. It grows the pot and makes money while I sleep.

Saving Interest

The one piece of advice I will give you about reducing your mortgage cost is this. Deposit your salary into a mortgage-offset account. Use this account to save for the deposit on your next property, and to pay off your credit card in full each month. If you have a $500k mortgage and $50k in a mortgage offset account, interest on your mortgage will only be calculated on $450k. That's a big deal.

If you lack the discipline to leave money sitting in an account like that, *and* you have a principal-and-interest loan, do this instead. Split your monthly mortgage payment in two and pay it fortnightly. A $500k mortgage over 30 years at 6.5% will cost you $3,160 a month, and $637,722 in interest. Pay $1,580 a fortnight instead (half of $3,160), and you'll pay off your mortgage six years earlier and save $146,869 in interest! That's a lot of money and time!

Negotiating a Tax Debt

I can't discuss the available options if you're outside Australia, but I know from personal experience that the Australian Taxation Office is very accommodating when it comes to outstanding debts.

There are two important provisos:

1. You must open a dialogue with them as soon as you know there's a problem. I know it isn't easy to call them and say, "Sorry to tell you this, but I'm in deep sh*t and can't pay you." Do it anyway.

2. Your debt stress must be genuine and you'll need to convince them of this. In my case, I gave them a copy of my divorce papers, my list of expenses and my income statements for the last six months.

When I got divorced, my finances took a real beating. Some of it manifested in a tax debt of around $15,000. I wrote to the Tax Office and explained my situation (using the evidence described above), and made a heartfelt plea for debt reduction.

To my surprise, they reduced it by 50%! They imposed a few conditions on the deal but I was more than willing to comply, and soon my tax debt was gone!

5 | MASTERING DEBT

Debt is like electricity.

You respect electricity because you know it can kill you.

Debt can do the same; it just takes longer.

Like electricity, debt can do amazing things. It can multiply capital, compress time and accelerate outcomes.

In other words, it can help you build an asset base with less of your own money, and get you to self-sufficiency (freedom) sooner. That's why it's called 'leverage'.

As Archimedes, the ancient Greek mathematician said,

"Give me a lever long enough and a fulcrum strong enough and, single-handedly, I will move the earth."

Debt can mean the difference between an extraordinary life and one filled with struggle and scarcity.

Your parents probably grew up believing that all debt was bad - "Never a borrower nor a lender be" - and that carrying debt was born out of necessity. It wasn't a strategy for wealth creation.

My parents could have built a substantial property portfolio and become wealthy in the process. Dad was an outstanding builder - fast, meticulous, and everything over-engineered. They owned their first home outright from day one, and each subsequent home from then on. They never had a mortgage their entire lives.

But despite these huge advantages, their fear of debt held them back, and they never owned a single investment property. They divorced in their 60's, and after selling the family home in a depressed market, emerged with less than $200k. It was a pittance after five decades of bone-crushing work.

Don't fear debt. Master it.

Fear holds people back, and the strongest driver is <u>ignorance</u>. Worse still, ignorance creates *imagined* fear, meaning decisions and actions have no basis in fact. They are *irrational*.

Whenever fear directs you, observe it and ask how much of it is coming from ignorance. If it *is*, get educated - not from friends of the family or someone's mate who just did x-y-z. Get it from those who've consistently succeeded doing what *you'd* like to do.

I can't stress this enough. People are lazy and they abdicate responsibility for their future to 'advisors' who don't have the runs on the board. When I want to learn a new skill, I always check to see what successes the teacher has had. If they're self-evident and provable, I'll listen. If they're prepared to help and advise me, I'll act on their advice. When someone asks my advice then ignores it or does the opposite, I won't offer it again. I don't have time to *convince* people to take it.

Good, Bad and Ugly Debt

Debt that's used to acquire income-producing growth assets that banks *like*, and where value can be added, is usually *good*.

Almost every other kind of debt is either bad or downright ugly.

Good Debt

An 80% loan on an appropriate-to-area residential real estate asset in a suburb with a proven history of capital growth *and* wages growth is generally *good debt*. Bit of a mouthful, I know.

Wages growth matters because it signals future investment in the area like renovations, redevelopment and gentrification of streets and parks and other public spaces.

'Appropriate-to-area' means the house fits into the style of the neighborhood. Avoid houses that are way too big compared to the others, or which push hard against the general design language of the established homes, unless there's an emerging trend towards that style in the area.

An example of a good debt might be a $560k loan on a $700k freestanding brick veneer home with enhancement potential in a middle ring suburb where capital growth and wages growth have trended up for at least a few years. Proximity to transport, schools, cafes and facilities are also key (though not *next door* to them).

Incidentally, a line of credit used for property acquisition falls into the same debt category. A line of credit to buy a boat **does not**.

Fewer than 10% of properties are investment-grade, so this type of debt comes with a few provisos that bear learning. Before you set out on your property investment journey, you MUST get yourself educated about the important principles of property selection.

Make sure you check the Additional Resources section of this book for related materials. Don't skip this; there's too much at stake to get it wrong. Armed with the right knowledge, though, you'll be ahead of 99% of your contemporaries.

Why is real estate so good for debt?

For the average person, no other investment offers the advantages of quality residential real estate. Here's why:

- You can control a $1,000,000 purchase with just $200k of your own money – even less at higher LVRs (loan-to-value-ratios) - though I prefer the conservative sleep-at-night approach.
- You can boost its value with things like paint, plants, a carport, fixtures, render, window furnishings, a light renovation, etc.
- The government will help you pay for it (depending on where you live) through tax concessions.
- A tenant will help you pay for it (via rent).
- You don't need to sell it to access some of its gains. Instead, you can obtain a line of credit, secured against the asset.
- You can use the equity to accumulate more properties, without selling up. NOTE: Only do this through a line of credit. Never allow a lender to cross-collateralize your properties (where they secure one purchase with multiple properties).
- A <u>carefully selected</u> real estate investment is far less volatile than most other investment-grade asset classes (including *speculative* real estate) because it's mostly driven by fundamentals.

There's a mountain of information on the subject of real estate investing. A lot of it is nonsense, too. The principles of real estate *investing* (not speculation) are fundamentally simple.

Whilst you do need to understand property selection, finance, taxation and so on, it isn't nearly as complicated or as scary as some will have you believe.

Likewise, it doesn't happen as quickly or magically as many others say, either. Like all worthwhile things, it requires a bit of time and education to make wise decisions, and to recognize a good deal when you see it.

In my view, *good debt* occupies a narrow subsection of this asset class. Nonetheless, when you consider the fact that most of the world's multi-millionaires hold (and grow) much of their wealth via real estate, it becomes obvious how important it is to learn this stuff.

Real estate is one of the few ways an average person can become wealthy, providing they make the effort to learn the ropes and they exercise the discipline to apply what they learn.

Bad Debt

Bad debt includes any instrument (personal loan, credit card, hire purchase, lease, line of credit) that's used to buy a depreciating asset.

The biggest offender is the recurring car buyer.

Spending $36,650 (including interest and fees) on a $30,000 car and justifying it as a tax perk is stupid, especially when you can buy a three-year-old one for $15,000.

Even if you pay cash for a car – and you should – you can still depreciate it and claim all the same running expenses, just as you would if you stumped up double the price on a new one with a loan. Also, you don't need a loan to claim a tax break and you sure as hell shouldn't use tax deductions as an excuse to spend more than necessary for a set of wheels.

The number of people who justify their vehicle updates with this nonsense is laughable. Many years ago I was one of them.

The most efficient way to buy a car is to get a 'last-in-the-series' (with all bugs and design issues resolved) pre-owned car of at least four years vintage, because it'll have had a lot of its depreciation hit by then. Buy it with a complete service history and, if possible, a one-owner example. Pay cash for it and keep it until it costs too much to maintain or it dies gracefully, whichever comes first.

At the time of writing, we own three cars with no debt. Together, they cost their first owners a combined total of almost $225,000. We paid $70,000 for all three of them (even though one is only two years old). I expect we'll have them for at least another five years – probably longer.

Credit Cards

Remember, debt for buying income-producing growth assets that appeal to banks, and where value can be added, is usually **good**.

But another *good* debt, believe it or not, is a credit card - but only if it has at least 30 interest-free days, and you use it correctly.

WARNING: If you lack the money or the discipline to pay your card off completely at the end of the interest-free period then this instrument is your enemy and you should stay away from it!

If you have the wisdom to know the effects of compounded stupidly-high interest rates, the maturity to act on that wisdom, and the discipline to snub 'new shiny' syndrome, then the credit card is a great tool for debt reduction and wealth creation. Here's why.

Reason One

You can deposit all your income into a mortgage offset account, pay all your bills with your credit card and only withdraw what you need from your offset account each month to pay off your card. This systematically reduces the amount upon which your mortgage interest is calculated – saving you interest costs. **It's free money.**

Remember, interest on your mortgage is calculated daily, so any extra money you have sitting in an offset account reduces the amount used to calculate the interest bill for the month. That's where the free money comes from.

Simply deposit all your income into the offset account, pay all your bills via credit card; then when the credit card bill falls due, pay it out in full (not the minimum payment) from your offset account. It's not that hard and it can save you tens of thousands of dollars.

Reason Two

Another huge benefit for the disciplined credit card user is the chance to accumulate points (assuming you get one with a rewards program, which you should). You simply exchange your points for cash back on your credit card balance. An alternative, which I love, is to exchange points for fuel cards or grocery store cards. **More free money!**

You might be tempted to save your points for a new shaver or a vacuum cleaner or an iPad, but don't. If you need to buy something, get the cash back on your card, then buy it on eBay or Amazon for a lot less than what your card provider charges to exchange points for products.

Trust me on this – you'll be far better off.

If you don't go for fuel cards or grocery cards, always exchange your points for cash-back, then buy your item from the cheapest source with your card again. This will earn you even more points and more free money. Woo-hoo!

Lifestyle Purchases

I'm a bloke, so I've always loved toys. Motorbikes, cars, four-wheel-drives, audio gear, photography gear - all of it! I even loved the smell of my Bowers & Wilkins speakers when I first brought them home...

But danger lurks here. If you don't use your head instead of your heart (or your adrenal gland, or whatever it is that makes us buy these things), toys will keep you broke!

The **only** way to buy them is with cash, (or cash deposited into your credit card *first*) and only when you can afford them! Let me explain.

Say you've been lusting after a $30,000 Harley. If you stick that money into an index fund earning 7.5% pa, it will turn into $133,825 in 20 years (or $282,646 in 30 years)! Alternatively, use that $30k as a 10% deposit on a $280k townhouse in the right area, and if it grows by an average of 6% pa, you'll have an asset worth $1,686,321 in 30 years, plus a raft of tax deductions.

That's a gross profit of $1.4 million!

Do you really *need* that brand new bike? Could you instead buy a $12,000 one and invest the difference? The money you spend today on any lifestyle product (boats, PWCs, motorbikes, holidays and tech gadgets) are all terrible applications for debt financing. Why? Well, like the car, they all depreciate quickly. The holiday does this instantly! Also, they don't produce any income, nor can you enhance their value. And if you want to recover any of their remaining equity, you have to sell the underlying 'asset'.

By the way, if you think a holiday house is an asset, in most cases, you'll be wrong. For one, banks hate lending against properties that have seasonal or holiday usage and their LVR (loan to value ratio) and interest rates will reflect this.

Second, the servicing and maintenance costs can be very high, eating into returns, while seasonal vacancies can be a real problem from a cash flow and security standpoint.

If you want a holiday house, rent one instead. Our family rents luxury multi-million dollar homes during the low season and we pay peanuts for the privilege. What's more, we stay in a different one each time. It beats the hell out of 'owning' one, that's for sure.

debt-free

Ugly Debt

The most crippling debt is any card you receive with an interest-free 'honeymoon' loan. These invariably carry obscene interest rates once the interest-free (or payment-free) period ends. The problem is, the long honeymoon lulls you into a false sense of prosperity, so you go and buy more stuff. Then when the interest payments finally kick in, you're in deep sh*t.

Commonly offered by retailers of white goods, furniture and electrical items, these loans can be hard to resist, especially when the Bosch 3-door fridge is screaming, "Take me home today!"

But once the honeymoon is over, you can find yourself with a large debt for something that was once new and shiny, but is now just another item on your list of financial burdens.

If you really need something, pay cash or buy a used one. Once, we needed a replacement dishwasher for an investment property. Instead of forking out for a new one, we got an almost-new $700 one off eBay for $200.

Avoid store cards and interest-free offers; indeed any type of consumer product loan with a honeymoon period. Get the whole idea out of your head and don't ask again.

6 | BREATHE AGAIN

Okay, we're almost at the end. If you've read this far, good on you for sticking around and hopefully, taking these ideas on-board. If you do, you'll be way ahead of most people.

And speaking of people, some will tell you that money's not important. But that's like telling a person who's dying of thirst that a glass of water isn't important. Money *is* important where money works - like living without stress, getting medical care, or doing work you love. It puts a roof over your head and food in your belly. It determines where you live, how warm you are in the winter and how much freedom you get to enjoy.

Likewise, many will say that money changes people. I think that's rubbish. I believe it *reveals* people. A good person who acquires a lot of money can do more good. A bad person becomes worse.

The theme throughout this book is simple. You **can** be debt-free and you *should* strive for it.

If you follow the steps you've just read, you will see daylight again. None of it is rocket science, and in terms of debt reduction, no further reading is required.

Once you're freed from the burden of debt, you can finally stop *dreaming* about a better life and start **planning** it instead. Wouldn't that be nice for a change?

You'll be able to plan your retirement with greater certainty, and delight yourself with believable daydreams about the other interests you're going to pursue when money is no longer a problem.

A lot of people will tell you to start with the end in mind (the big picture), but I reckon it's much easier to have those thoughts after you've proven you can take the first few steps. When you see the outcome of those steps, the big picture snaps into focus automatically.

Killing off debt (at least the kind that applies to depreciating goods) is empowering, and it delivers a new lease on life that's impossible to see when you're neck deep in the quagmire.

Get out of your own way, ditch the excuses, and start executing. I guarantee your life will take on a lustre that's been missing for years. You'll finally be able to breathe again.

debt-free

A Final Word *(Warning)*

"Man sacrifices his health in order to make money. Then he sacrifices money to recuperate his health. And then he is so anxious about the future that he does not enjoy the present; the result being that he does not live in the present or the future; he lives as if he is never going to die, and then dies having never really lived."

The Dalai Lama

A Small Favor

Thank you so much for reading this book. I honestly hope it helps you to kill your debts and live a better life. If you follow my advice, you *will* kill off your debts and we'll both be glad we met.

But if you want to go further and really master your money, I urge you to read the items listed on the next page. Together, they will help you to spend wisely, find more time, invest fearlessly and set yourself up for the rest of your days.

My goal with this book is to help as many people get out from under and start enjoying life again. If you have some suggestions on how I can do that more effectively, I'd love to hear about them. Please email me anytime at the address below.

Also, see which projects I'm working on at https://peterfritz.co.

And finally, can you do me a favor? If you've found this book to be helpful, could you please leave a quick and honest review on Amazon? And please tell others who might benefit, too. Debt ruins a lot of lives, and I know this little book can make a difference if people read it and follow the process I've outlined.

Thank you again, and good luck with your own reinvention!

Peter Fritz
pf@peterfritz.co

Additional Resources

Great Books Worth Reading

How To Grow A Multi-Million Dollar Property Portfolio in Your Spare Time | Michael Yardney

The Millionaire Next Door | Thomas Stanley & William Dank

Unshakeable - Your Financial Freedom Playbook | Tony Robbins

Useful Downloads

https://peterfritz.co/equity (Home Equity Calculator)
https://peterfritz.co/expenses (Sample Expenses Spreadsheet)

My Web Sites

https://officeanywhere.co - Work and Live on Your Terms
https://midlifetribe.com - Midlife Mastery for Trailblazers
https://peterfritz.co - My home base

Disclaimer

I'm not a psychologist, and I'm not a financial advisor. This material doesn't constitute financial advice but rather, a collection of personal opinions based on my own experiences.

The recommendations I make are the same ones I make to my own family and friends because they've worked for me.

When it comes to financial matters, you should obviously consult with a suitably qualified professional who has your financial success as their first priority (known as a fiduciary).

About the Author

Peter Fritz is the founder of midlifetribe.com, a place where midlifers can learn how to reinvent themselves in their 'second act'.

More recently, he launched officeanywhere.co, offering inspiration and practical advice on working remotely - something he's done for decades. His focus is on helping people to live and work on their terms. He's also a dad, a husband, an *ex-husband*; a photographer and outdoorsy guy.

He started Midlife Tribe in his late 40's when he realized there were scores of people in the same age group facing similar challenges and asking the same questions. Like many, he had his *own* midlife crisis, and a rapidly diminishing time-frame to get his money sorted was a big part of it.

He didn't get a Harley or a mistress, but he *did* splurge on other things in an effort to fill the void that appeared. He survived it all and went on to create a life many of us seek. Killing off debt was an important part of that process.

Today, he enjoys a good life, but getting there required screwing up in all the areas that count (relationships, money, health and work/life balance); and learning what works and what doesn't.

He consults for companies in a diverse range of industries both locally and abroad, and lives with his wife and son, and just down the road from his two daughters (above).

debt-free

Glossary of Fancy Words

Modeling - Mimicking or copying someone/something else.

Recurring Expenses - The kind that come every week/month/year.

Compounded - In the case of debt, it is interest that's calculated on the initial principal and also on the accumulated interest of previous periods of a deposit or loan. It's interest on interest. With an investment, this is VERY GOOD. With a loan, it's bad. It's the 8th wonder of the world.

CSV File - Stands for Comma-Separated Values. Each value is separated with a comma. In a spreadsheet, it's ugly.

Surplus - Any extra amount left over.

Delayed Gratification - The act of waiting for stuff you really want until you can actually afford it.

Unsecured - In the case of debts, the lender has no right to take any assets away from you if you don't repay them. E.g. Credit cards.

Garnishee - A third party (you) who is instructed by way of legal notice to surrender money to settle a debt or claim. It's money that's taken straight from your income to settle a debt, whether you like it or not.

LVR (Loan to Value Ratio) - The amount you're borrowing as a percentage of the value of the property being used as security for the loan. The lower the LVR, the lower the risk is to the bank. If you buy a $600,000 property and borrow $480,000, your LVR is 80%.

Depreciation - A reduction in the value of an asset over time. Most consumer goods depreciate. Good investments do the opposite; they *appreciate*.

www.ingramcontent.com/pod-product-compliance
Lightning Source LLC
Chambersburg PA
CBHW072016230526
45468CB00021B/1604